UP NORTH BIG CITY STREET

Published Books by Zack Gilbert

My Own Hallelujahs
Up North Big City Street

UP NORTH
BIG CITY STREET

Poetry
by
Zack Gilbert

PATH PRESS, INC.
Chicago

Library of Congress Cataloging-in-Publication Data

Gilbert, Zack, 1925–
    Up north big city street.

    I. Title.
PS3557.I3423U6 1986   811'.54   86-23292
ISBN 0-910671-09-5
ISBN 0-910671-10-9 (pbk.)

Published by Path Press, Inc., 53 West Jackson Blvd.
Chicago, Illinois 60604

Distributed by Chicago Review Press, 814 North Franklin Street, Chicago, Illinois 60610

Internal Book Design by Janet Cheatham Bell

Jacket cover Design by Chuck Rice

Manufactured in the United States of America

Dedicated to all the beautiful gals and guys
Around 79th & Halsted street and other black
Southside locations.

STATEMENT

This is not an apology for writing *Big City Street*. However, before I decided to have it published, I did go through much soul searching. I knew that there were some whose sensitivities would be offended because of the street language used and the apparent negative images of some of the characters. But trying to be as authentic and realistic as possible in my portrayal of these characters, I had no other choice.

Perhaps most of you understand that whenever a writer puts pen to paper in an attempt to depict a people in a particular time and place and circumstance, there is always a risk of concerned criticism. Even sometimes harsh and angry. It should also be understood that in writing about these somewhat socially tarnished characters, I am not endorsing them as role models. On the contrary, I am merely saying that they exist and are also entitled to a sympathetic voice. Of course, I assume that most of you understand this.

Therefore, without any further comment, I give you, *Up North Big City Street*.

The Author
Chicago, Illinois
March 1986

PART ONE

PORTRAITS OF THE PEOPLE

TINA BACK IN ACTION

Free of her pads
And recent blood
Her yeasty body glows.
She is sun radiant,
Earthy,
Rock strong,
Willow supple.

Ready,
She strolls hurricane
Into the "Glass House."

DOBBY ON THE PROWL

He walks beneath
The cold blood lights
In the ice cube neon signs.
Struts into the steam bath
Of hot bodies, laughter
And the loud bouncing boom.
Cat like he stool crawls
Eyeing a possible conquest
While deep in his need
Want spreads like a
Week old hunger.

EARNESTINE

Behind the bar
Over the mirrowed wall
At the "Jazz Hut"
Are pictures.
One is Earnestine's.
Of all the bar maids
Here she is the most alive.
A honey bee of zing and zip
And dash and daring.
Swift music made soft woman.
The best drink in the house.

She knows how to evade
The pass and keep the friend,
How to say no
With maybe in her voice.

"HOG HEAD"

He waddles in,
This stubby, brown man
Pushing fifty,
Trying to make all
The young babes
With his easy
Going bread.
Buying promises.

They say his wife
Is afraid to ask him
For food money
And his children
Are afraid to ask him
For carfare.

To his face
These broads all
Blush and call him
"Sweet Charlie,"
Behind his back
He is "Hog Head."

TODAY WE WATCH
THE PACKERS AND BEARS

It is no accident
That we crash
Head on head
And bone on bone.
Is this His great
Design to keep us
Busy bruising
Each other?
Does he reach
A climax
When we kill?

Today we watch
The Packers
And Bears
On television.
We feel a wild,
Exhilarating
Warmness
In our balls
When they fuck
Each other up.

THE GAMBLER

Cards are his
Conjure man
Full of
Ju'ju magic
Kids and wife
Can wait.

A whirlwind
In his brain
A racer
In his blood
It is
His whiskey high
It is
His cocaine sniff
His heroin fix
His orgasm
His woman.

Kids and wife
Can wait.

DELORES

Delores, the dried up
Prune, pours your special
Drink with clumsy quickness.
She is a worrisome rapper,
This thin weed.
Loves herself.
Reality is a mirror
She can't face,
A door she'll never
Open.

All evening she
Struts behind the bar
Of her imagined importance
Waiting for the man
Who will take her
And her kids and bills

And see her as she
Never was or will be
Through the untruths
Of her eyes.

SISTER LILLIE

When sister Lillie
From the South Halsted
Street Fellowship
Church come asking
We all give.
Even the drunks
And dope addicts,
The pimps and whores,
The hard working
People.

Word of mouth
Talk done made
Her legit.
Word of mouth
Talk says she
Really looks out
For the needy.

LUCINDA

Sometimes you be
All the sassy little girls
I've known.
Nose in the air.
Again you be
Trusting woman,
Long years of living
Understanding.
You blues and gospel,
Jazz and pop songs,
You down home church
Shouter
And up north
Big city street
Dancer.
You touch that
Deep inside of me
Place
Few folks know
I have.

ONE NIGHT AT THE BLACKROOM

For Jo Ann

Tall and willowy,
You sit aloof
In your tigress repose,
Thinking.
The music showers
Your stillness with
It's screaming sound.
Others move around gaily
Shaking luscious fannies.
But you, cool as
The stone of your eyes,
Are the epitome of
Sensuality
In the closets
Of my mind.

THE FAT LADY

*(Old saying: "You ain't fat
                You justa pleasing plump.")*

The fat lady softly
Talking her tensions out,
Round and roly-poly fat
But smelling of freshness
And just a subtle whisp
Of the best cologne.
She chats with a hint of
The highest priced gin in
The house on her breath.

Bending toward me
She is a voluptuous
Rise of brown flesh.
Laughs sedately, sips
Her gin as her big eyes
Show visions of bedrooms.

SALLY'S PLEASURE

When I asked her
Why I couldn't see her
More often she said,
"You pleasure, honey.
That's why. My other man
Gimme things. Helps me.
That's why I sees him when
He wants me. But you pleasure,
Honey. And lately ain't
Been able to 'ford
My pleasure much."

SHAKEY'S VOW

"Yeah man ahm
Gonna quit drinking,"
Shakey said,
"After last night
Ah know ah gotta
Put it all down.
Man, ah saw rats
Jumping outta wine bottles,
Saw spiders big as peoples
Crawling up and down the walls,
Saw little pink elephants playing
Leap-frog on the ceiling.
Felt the blood cells in my blood
Doing the bump. Ah ain't lieing man
That stuff done really get t'me.
Lately ah don't want no woman
No matter how young N fine.
Yeah man, ah don't want nothing but booze
N ah ain't particular see. Rot gut,
Cheap wine, you name it, ah'll claim it.
But ah'm gonna put it all down, man."

"Yeah, someday he'll stop drinking,"
        Lefty said,
"When he stretched out stone, cold dead."

LEFTY TO MAUDE

Say honey
Yo ain't sexy
Sitting thar on that
Bar stool wid yo
Dress up high
Showing them fat
Peas and beans
And collard green thighs.

You musta think
Yo thang a slice
Of sweet potato pie.

A VISITOR FROM CITY HALL

After winning the
Election the alderman
Came back to see us
As he said he would.
He bought drinks and
Shook hands as if he
Was still running
For office.
He said he was going
To fight the machine
As he had promised.
We couldn't believe
Our eyes.
We had never seen
A politician up in
Heah
After an election.

MR. SMITH:

—Our Friendly Undertaker

He has grown rich
Planting seeds
That will never grow.
He lays them out
All spruced up.
Most
Dressed better
In death
Than ever in life.
Nothing is too good
For the dearly departed
He'll tell you.

Spend joyfully
On this once
In a life time
Trip.

BABY SUE

She knows
No Latin or Greek.
Can't even speak English
Very well
If you get what I mean.
The street is her good book
The bar is her bible.

I feel sorry
For the dude
Who tries to pull wool
Over her big, brown eyes.

He is in for
A hell of a kick
In the pants surprise.

FROM "LONGFOOTS"

Man ah know
You done heard
'Bout jamming Johnny.
He the cat that got
That hit record
"Slipping N sliding."
Man he uh big dood.
But he don't act
Like big.
He beautiful.
Ah knowed him down
Home in 'Sippi
N seeing him at
The High Chapparell
Ah thought he was
Gonna act uppity
You know.
But he gave me
One of those big
Cotton pickin' hugs
N took me wid
Him after the show
N treated me
Like ah wuz jus'
As big uh hit
As he wuz.

Man you know
He still likes
Wild greens
N conebread.

RUBY

On Her "Happy Hours" Time

Sometimes she
Really
Gets with it
When the funky
Mellow music
Slides around
The dreamy corners
Of her mind.
Her Gladys
Knight voice,
Rich and troubled
As blues,
Grabs you hard
With its magic
And won't let go.

Then you see
Her as never
Before.
Grapefruit tiddies,
Sugar cane waist,
Cantaloupe hips
Talking
Nitty gritty
Moving, moving
Gutty, gutty deep
Down moving.

LITTLE FOXY ROXY

Little foxy Roxy
Together as can be
Little foxy Roxy
Once was sweet on me
Gave me love and kisses
For free free free.

Little foxy Roxy
Love turned to ice
Little foxy Roxy
Who was once so nice
Can't get her love now
Even for a price.

LEFTY TO LONGFOOTS:

"Man, they it."

Man doncha
Mess wid them
Two broads over there.
They funny.
You know what I mean.
But they also beautiful.
I mean they got uh
Beautiful thang going.
Treat each otha wid
Mo respect than
Most husbands and wives.
Jus look at that love
In they eyes
For each other.
How they touch,
Softly.
Like words and music
Coming to uh perfect
Understanding.
Man, they it.

ONCE UPON A TAVERN TIME

Once upon a tavern time
Once upon a booze house jump
Everybody feeling fine
Snapping fingers, doing the bump.

Sally turns her jollies on
Buddy gets his juices up
Jojo rubber to the bone
Flo can't shake her hips enough.

>Cats and foxes having fun
>Doing they thang from
>Dust to dawn
>Jumping, jamming each
>And everyone.

Look at Dodo doing the split
Dig Cool Papa's strutting glide
Everybody doing they bit
With salty rhythm, funky pride.

>Cats and foxes having fun
>Doing they thang from
>Dust to dawn
>Jumping, jamming each
>And everyone.

MARIE

Her eyes
Are sad moons
Searching the taverns
Of the night.
Drunk on wine
And music
They seek out
The ready men.
Her face,
Once a snapshot
Of innocence,
Is now a canvas
Of experience,
Wise to the night
As the mother owl
Who sits
In her tree top
And scoffs
At the world.

EVENING SCENE

She was fine
Creamy brown
Curvaceous slim
And sexy.

He was just
An ordinary dude.
But the macho in him
Saw unconditional
Surrender in her eyes
       (Instead of dollar signs.)

And when they got
To the place they called
The killing floor
       (And she asked him for the dough)
Hurt and surprise
Crippled his speech;
Brought grown man blues
To his bleeding eyes.

LITTLE MAMA:

Our favorite Barmaid

Little mama
Is not little
Anymore.
Her hips are two
Stuffed pillows
And her tiddies are
Blown up carnival
Ballons.
And yet, she
Featherfoots behind
The bar,
Her moves still
Young and full
Of bubbles and bounce;
Her concern
A honey cup of
Understanding.

PLAYERS

They meet here
Once a week,
This thin
Pumpkin colored
Woman and this
Stocky walnut
Colored man.

They sit quietly
Over in the booth
Making love wid
They eyes.

You can tell
They aint married.
That is, not
To each other.

CORNER PIMP

From Longfoots

He super pimp.
Yeah him over there,
Lining up those
Over the hill bitches
Playing his slick
Con game.
He works hard,
For sure,
This corner cutter
Making his
Pennies
The hard way.

MARTHA AT THE SOFT SHOE LOUNGE

Let's go Emma
I can't stand this place
These dim eyed women
Fumbling in the fog.
The music is rich and good, yes
But the people are sick,
The people are foul.

Let's go Emma
I can't stand these men
Unloving these unlovable women
And flaunting their sex
Like a weapon in the hand.
They see you through eyes
Greedy with glitter.

Let's go Emma
There must be another place
On some not too far away street
Where we can have a taste and talk
And relax our weariness
After a hard day's work
At the factory.

LANA BROADSTREET

Your truth is more truth
Than the church sister
With holy water in her veins.
You, facer of facts,
Wise street walker
Whose home is the single bars.
No hypocrite here
Like the sheltered housewife
Who gives it up
For what she says is love.
But you, honest as
Hard work and rain,
Put it on the line
For the indiscriminate dollar.

FROM LEFTY /

/ Encouraging words to Pete
Before his expected
Prison sentence

They can't keep
You in there, Lil'brothah
No nevah.
Can they keep uh
Fish outa watah
Can they keep
Candy from uh baby
Can they keep uh
Bananah from uh monkey
Uh fix from uh junkie
Black pungtang
From uh honky
Uh sale from uh jew
Uh bad nigger foot
From uh high priced shoe?

Can they keep you
From going back home
To see yo mamah
In Alabamah
Can they keep uh
Stuttering man
From his stammah
Uh sleepy man from napping
Uh toothless man from smacking
Uh leaving woman from packing
Uh pocket picker from yo pocket

Uh country preacher from his hollah
Uh hustling bitch from yo dollah

Can they keep uh rabbit
From outa the brier patch,
Brothah? Don't worry, you'll
Be outta there N back
In no time.

MAYBE NEXT TIME

We wonder
Why he comes
In here so often
And read his poems.
Sometimes we say
He crazy but we
Know he aint.
His poems cut deep
Into our guts,
Make us mad.
Especially at
White folks.

If he gonna
Turn us boiling
And leave us
So helpless
Maybe next time
Better he bring
Guns.

BAR CYNIC

One by one
We go
Back to
The dust.

Tick by tick
We fly
Back to our
Natural state.

The lie
Is the now
This flesh and blood
We breathe in.

Before
And after
The heartbeat
Is truth.

SOME WOMEN AT "THE HAPPY HOLE" LOUNGE

They are all
Up in heah,
The embalmed living
Sitting at the bar,
Marble eyes staring
Into nowhere.

Once their moves
Were electric,
Their bodies quick
As a sudden zig zag
Of lightning,
Their faces bright
As the noon
Of June sunshine.

But now they are
Grave yard junk,
Full of stink
And little or
No motion.

THOSE MANY WHO NEVER DROP IN

Look up from your
Drink sometimes,
Buddy Boy,
And watch them pass
By the window,
Those many who never
Drop in.
Those head high
Holders
And straight step
Walking women.

Look on them
And be happy
That their needs are never
Up in heah.

BIG FLO

Her stomach sits
Like a globe
Between her thighs
And her tiddies
Are two bowling pins
Hanging.

Speaking of woman flesh
Desired
She is waste.

But there is wisdom
In her seldom smile,
Cool logic
In her eyes.

REV. MOHN

He preaches hard,
This son of God
With the big Cadillac.

Throws his head back
And shouts in claps
Of thunder.

Sisters tremble
Beneath his strong
Hallelujahs.

Some relive other
Special secret times,
Remembering the holy rod.

KEEPING THE PEACE

From Good Kid

When the stranger
Came up in heah
Talking against drinking
Booze
And eating hog meat
The owner had 'em
Thrown out into the street.
He also said something
About all white folks
Were devils
And I think Curtis said
He knowed that was a lie
'Cause he was acquainted
With some good white folks.
Anyway we were glad
When he left 'cause
He made us uneasy.

You see we all up
In heah
Like to do our little
Drinking in peace.

JOINING THE ESTABLISHMENT

From Buddy Boy

Turn into the monstah.
Be like 'em.
Be uh bad muthah
Be no othah cheek turnah
Do in befo you don in.
This is the only
Way fur survival.
Always me fust
N' you latah
Be uh big, fat dollah
Grabbah
Try to get funky rich
Quick quick
Piss on the po
We all grown
N' we kno
The sco.
Children's games ovah
Get yo hard up.
Fuck 'em fust.

LEFTY TO HOGHEAD:

(After reading articles in a
Chicago newspaper praising a few
Hand-picked middle-class Blacks.)

"Hey looka heah
At this shit
In the white folk's
Paper.
Don't yall know
Yall middle class
Now?
Living in split
Level bungalows
Wid manicured lawns
'N sending yo children
To private schools.
Yall got
Two cars in every
Garage
'N making ovah
Twenty grand
Uh yeah.
Hey, yall arrived
Now.
Aint yo po asses
Happy?
Looka heah
See yall.
Charley says so."

JOSHUA

Joshua read about
That bloody weekend
Like everybody else.
And being human,
It sent a cold blade
Of ice up and down
His spine.
But he had a family
To feed.
So he went to his
Night job as always,
Caught the bus going
And coming back.
Then, in the
Two blocks on
His way home
From the bus stop,
Somebody blew
His life away
For two dollars
45 cents,
And a CTA bus
Token.

CUTE CUSTARD CONNIE

Wispy
Waiting
Wasp
Curved and
Compact.
Everything
Any woman got
But more
Concentrated.
"Best things
Come in little
Packages,"
She'll brag.
Cute
Custard
Connie—
But not for
Free.

CRUEL WOMAN

From Jojo

Yo wind chill
Factor
Is thirty below
Zero
Cold woman.
Bad as that hawk
Outside
Wid two razors
In each hand
Evil woman
Wid
Ice water blood
Icicle fingers
Ice cube lips.
Yo voice,
A bruising
Bitter wind;
Yo thighs
Ice slabs in a
No thawing river.
Aint yo name,
February
Chicago,
Cruel woman?

MAYBELLE

That idiot box
On the wall
Where the soap operas
Live is more real
To her than she is.
It is her tranquilizer,
Her therapeutic jack off.
It is her breath and blood.

It is better than chains
Or whips or guns for the man
Because it is considered,
By most people,
Legal.

EBONY WOMAN:
IN SUMMER AS YOU WALK

In summer
As you walk the southside
Streets of Chicago

I can see you strolling
Along the banks
Of the Kamby Bolongo

An African rhythm
Moving deep
Inside the curves
Of your loins

And the equator
Night stars
Glowing in the dark
Beauty of your eyes.

WHEN SHORTY SINGS THE BLUES

When Shorty sings the blues
Everybody gotta sit up and listen
When Shorty sings the blues
Everybody gonna be moved
Oh yeah,
Everybody gonna be grooved
When Shorty sings the blues.

His eyes they flash like lightning
His hands they clap like thunder
His voice is a groaning grumbling growl
That grabs and takes you under
It's spell.
When he sings the blues
Yeah, everybody gonna be moved.
      He groans,
"Baby don't you take my money and
Spend it on another man
Baby don't you take my money and
Spend it on another man
'Cause honey if you do
I'm gonna hurt you if I can."
      He grumbles,
"I aint fattening frogs for snakes
I aint raising tatters for hogs
I aint trading hoes for rakes
I aint raising cats for dogs."
      And growls,
"So baby you better
Better be straight with me
So baby you better
Better be straight with me

'Cause I aint gonna pay for
What another man's getting free."

Shorty always brings the house down
Hard
When he sings the blues.

FOR MORE POSITIVE BROTHERS

This is also a
Part of us.
Another corner
Of blackness.
Whether we want
To face up
To this truth
Or not.
This is also us
Here on this
Corner
In this place.
These people laughing,
Dancing, boozing,
Brawling.
Go to them more
Positive brothers.
Go to them
Before you write
Them off.
Go to them.
Teach and
Learn.

PART TWO

<u>**PERSONAL NOTES:**</u>
A Study In Moods

I have swallowed most of
The world religions like pills
And these have helped me
No more than my tranquilizers.

I CANNOT HEAR

Once my world was
More than skeletons,
Dead trees in the cold rain.
Time had not soured my taste
And my tongue dripped at the
Thought of candy and yams.
Sunrises were the bright rouge
Of young country girls
Trying to be women.
And the stars were dancing
Eyes of believing children
On Christmas eve.

Now street sounds speak to me
In voices of brass.
And when the dying cry for help
I cannot hear.

TO THE END OF THE STARS

It takes more and more
Alcohol to quiet these nerves
That are charged electric wires
In the flesh; hot little threads
Twisting its evil way.

Those who condemn
Show me an easier way to peace
And I will take it.

I have swallowed most of
The world religions like pills
And these have helped me
No more than my tranquilizers.

Show me the way and I
Will travel your road
Even to the end of the stars.

THE MELODY OF LAUGHTER

There are too many circles now
And too many back roads,
Too many streets I do not wish
To travel again.
Time doubles back into its agony
And the once joy song is sad,
Heavy as a blues without promise.

Space has narrowed into crowded
Tenement houses
As my time has grown short
And my memories long.

I cannot write beauty into my song again.
I have forgotten the melody of laughter.

YOUNG LOVERS

The young lovers over
In the booth disturb me.
Not because they are in love
But because they are still
Young enough to believe.

The music to them
Is a fire healer.
The whiskey is warm
Sunlight in the glass.

To me the music is
Like old folks talking
In lost tongues.
The whiskey, last years
Rain water in rank
Fruit jars.

When they dance their
Moves become magic.

I hurt deep in my bones
When I watch them.

CHANGES

The fluid dancers
Suddenly lose their cool
And are frantic

The soft music
Goes out of control
And becomes
A scream

And so does your voice
On the phone
Before you hang up
With a crash

Unexpectedly
Like the foolish doings
Of a child.

MY MIND IS NOT IN THIS SPACE

Tonight I am quiet
And you ask me why
I am unhappy.

I cannot tell you that
I am filled to the brim
With peace
Here in this loudness

My mind is not in this space
It is in another where

As I see these slick women
And cunning men. Turning
From the hurrying music

I remember green banks
And bright rivers,
A caught fish dancing
In sunlight.

SOMETIMES A FEELING COMES

Sometimes a feeling comes
Visiting at the perfect time.
It is a poem that you have felt
But could not write before.
Music without sound that had played
On the periphery of your mind.
A love in a far off future from the past.

You enjoy this visitor for that special while
Knowing you will never be able
To tell how it really was.

CITY RAINBOW

Bright hale of colors
Over the bleak buildings
After the rain,
You rise, an illusion,
As ghost are
At noon time,
You, a childhood thing,
Insulting my adult years;
A dead dream
As Christ or Santa Claus,
Competing with
Bricks and stone;
Hard eyed women,
Tight lipped men,
And death.

TONIGHT I WALK THROUGH THE STREETS

Tonight I walk through the streets
After hearing the crime stories told
But my ears are quiet to this terror.
The watching stars are my friends
And the moon is my faithful godmother.
Tonight I trust shadows that might kill,
Dark alleys that might consume me.
Other nights I may fear.
But tonight I have the power.
Invisible giants walk with me.

LOUD AND CLEAR

Once I did not
Understand your love.
I did not know that
Love could be a quiet thing.
Soft music at evening time.
I was always close to the loud,
The driving rhythms of express
Way traffic at rush hour;
Fast trains moving in the night.

Then you came with your whisper.
Now, after years of listening,
I hear you loud and clear.

YOU ASKED ME FOR SONGS

You asked me for songs
But my heart is dry
And fragile
As autumn leaves,
And my spirit is a
Dying tree
Afraid of the coming cold.

Where were you when
I was a young and straight willow,
And my leaves were tender and greener
Than April grass?

I do not have the magic
To return to spring,
And winter is not
The best companion
For your young dream.

—Zack Gilbert.